Finding UP

Linda Anthony Hill

Hill House Publishing

Acknowledgements

My first teacher and mentor about learning and dealing with life was my father, Robert William Anthony Sr. He was orphaned at age eleven and he and his sister made their way in a world not meant for orphans. He didn't earn a degree, but in a time when most people didn't go to college at all, the fact he attended Antioch was a big deal. When he died he was a VP at General Electric. I am always amazed by his life.

I'd also like to acknowledge Walter Burnett. He was my first teacher/employer in the art and science of dental technology. More than that he taught me how to work hard for something you want. He had grown up during the depression and it showed in the way he treasured the little things. It was my pleasure to apprentice with him.

My last mentor was Alan C. Walter who taught me some of what's contained in this book. He was a hard task-master with a gentle soul who taught me so much more than what I've written here. One of the last things he asked of me was to share the knowledge. That's what this book is about. He was a good friend and like the others, I miss him.

Last but, by all means, not least, my brother, Robert W. Anthony Jr. Since we were children, Rob has had a special talent for finding UP. I consider him with both admiration and a touch of jealousy. He is an inspiration.

Dedicated to

Cynthia Holsclaw-Francis and Del Hill

Table of Contents

"However difficult life may seem, there is always something you can do and succeed at." Stephen Hawking

Chapter 1

Absence and Presence

We live in a fast-paced world of people who seem to know where they're going, but in reality, most of them don't know which way is up. They should be climbing a staircase of experience and knowledge, but they don't know which steps lead up. What should their next goal be? Do they have a goal? How did they choose it, or did someone else choose it for them?

This first chapter is about Absence and Presence. We're going to explore them both and see what they really mean.

When I was forty-two my husband of eighteen years was diagnosed with stage four cancer. He had served in Vietnam with the Marine Corps and had been exposed to Agent Orange. No one considered the connection at that time.

On Thanksgiving Day, he died after being in a hospital for a month and in treatment for about four months.

My husband and I had been happily married with a thirteen-year-old daughter, a house (with a mortgage), two cars (with car notes), and a typical life. We were not prepared (I was not prepared) for this eventuality.

Our future was laid out. We/ I knew what the future looked like. We would grow old together. We would retire. He would fish. I would sew. We would sit in the evenings on the porch and watch the sunset from our matching rocking chairs. It was like a movie I could see in my mind.

Our life was like a building we had created together from scratch. And that building came crashing down on me that Thanksgiving Day in nineteen-ninety-six. I was in shock for months. Someone pointed out to me in March that it might be time to take the Christmas decorations down. I didn't even know I had Christmas decorations up. I was oblivious. I was Absent.

I got up every day and went to work at my business. I kept my daughter fed and clothed. But I was just going through the motions while avoiding the E-motions. E-motions are just Energy in motion. If you're avoiding your emotions you're not moving. If you want your energy to be in motion, you have to experience your emotions. That's often easier said than done.

We're told in many books and seminars to set goals and reach for them, but how do we set those goals? How do we decide what is the exact right next step? Could there be a formula? You know, like learning Math. First, we learn the numbers themselves, putting order into the Chaos. Then we learn the concepts of each number. Then we learn to add the numbers, then subtract, and so on. It's a formula for learning and it works.

But how does that apply to your job? How does it apply to someone whose whole life has collapsed on them? How does it apply to learning in general? Because learning is what we're ultimately talking about. Every new thing you want to do or try involves learning. Even dealing with a dreadful loss.

If you want to start investing in the stock market you'd better be prepared to learn about the market, about how to assess a company and its stock, about puts and calls and futures. Where do you start? Is there a formula that applies to learning about the stock market?

Every subject you attempt to master is subject to the same basic formula. I learned this formula from Alan C. Walter a couple of years after my husband died. Alan's books fill a small library in a ranch in North Texas called The Advanced Coaching and Leadership Center. His courses have changed thousands of lives. He helped me when I lost my way after my husband died. He was a genius. (Alan, not my husband, though my husband was pretty special in his own right. My husband's formula was; get up, go to work, stop at the pub, go home. Fish on weekends after the lawn was taken care of.)

In this book, I will explain a couple of concepts I learned from him (Alan) about learning. Once you know how to learn you can master anything you put your mind to. How many times have you given up on a subject or job or career because you became frustrated with it to the point of anger? Or just frustrated? Had you only known that anger is a third of the way up the staircase, and all you had to do was push through it without hurting anyone, you might have been able to get past it and push on through to success.

Instead, because we're taught as children that anger is bad, so when we encounter it, we throw up our hands and quit. We quit because we've learned that a particular emotion is "bad." Let me set this straight: Anger is healthy. All emotions are healthy, even the ones that don't feel good. Anger is merely a signpost. Learn to embrace your anger in order to let go of it and move up the staircase to the next step.

Let's look at the staircase. It has a daunting number of steps and each one must be used. Unfortunately, we start at the bottom. Actually, we start on the ground at absent. We are not even on the staircase. We lack any useful knowledge of the new (to us) subject.

When I lost my husband, I had been in the Green Zone, but the loss caused me to crash all the way to absence. It was like the childhood game of shoots and ladders. I didn't know what to do or where to turn.

I found the first step on the staircase is Presence. We have to become Present with the subject and in the world of the living. We have to look at it and become familiar with it. Steps can be climbed very quickly or very slowly depending on the complexity of the subject and our personal feelings about the subject. For instance, learning to use a pencil will not take as long as learning to fly a jet.

Same steps, we just have to stay on each step longer for the jet.

We may even have to break the jet down into smaller staircases, frequently revisiting the Red Zone and achieving the Green Zone.

Why do you think Pilots and Doctors and Lawyers and a host of other professionals are so confident in themselves? They've had more successes than the average person.

When you have Mastered a myriad of subjects you are no longer average in anything. You know from experience what it takes to Master a new subject. You are a winner.

Do yourself a favor. Right now, take out paper and pen and write a list of every subject you have Mastered. Be generous. Walking counts. Reading counts. If you're a safe driver, driving counts. Make the list as long as you can. You're not going to show it to anyone.

The longer the list, the more confident you should feel. This is not the time for humility. What have you succeeded at? What have you Mastered?

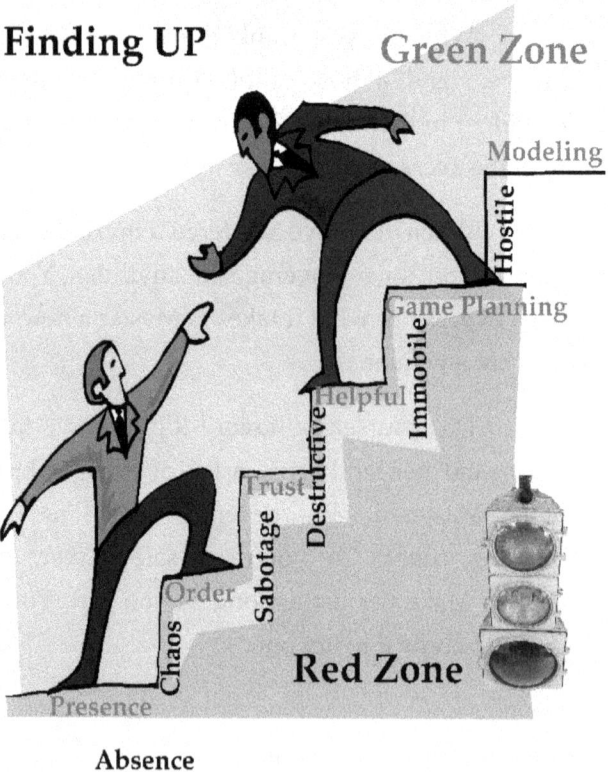

Finding UP

Green Zone

Modeling

Hostile

Game Planning

Immobile

Helpful

Destructive

Trust

Sabotage

Order

Chaos

Red Zone

Presence

Absence

32 Steps to Mastery-- 1 through 12

Spend some time on this. It will be worth it. Add to it every time you master a new subject. Feel the confidence swell.

What does it mean to be Present? Have you ever talked to someone who was there physically, but for your purposes there was no one there? You can tell when someone isn't there with you. It's one thing to be physically Present. It's quite another to be fully Present. To be fully Present, you must be right here, right now. If you're reading this and thinking of what you're going to do tomorrow afternoon then you aren't really here, are you?

So, showing up isn't enough. You have to show up mentally. You have to be paying attention. You have to care about what you're doing. If not, your body may be there, but YOU are Absent.

In this day of instant connection and instant communication, we are often somewhere else. I can't stress enough how important it is to be where you are, when you are, doing what you're doing while you're doing it.

There is no one thing you can do that will advance your life, your career, your relationships, and your happiness more than this. BE HERE NOW!

Your associates will appreciate it. Your boss will appreciate it. Your spouse will appreciate it. Your kids will appreciate it. Need I go on? Get Present. No matter where you are on the staircase, be present first and foremost.

"To succeed, you need to find something to hold on to, something to motivate you, something to inspire you." Tony Dorsett

Chapter 2

Chaos and Order

Given a pencil, a baby will immediately put it in its mouth. The baby is gaining valuable information in one of the only ways available to it. Babies and toddlers put everything in their mouth. It's how they move through the Chaos.

Whatever the subject, the next step is Chaos. Imagine walking into the cockpit of a plane or, just remember sitting for the first time in the driver's seat of a car. It's Chaos. There are dials and switches and handles and buttons. And what the h!!l is a PRNDL? Some people think of this as a negative step. In fact, all Red Zone steps and Yellow Zone steps are negative. Just as all Green Zone steps are positive. That doesn't mean you should, or even can, skip over them. They are, actually, the upward movement toward the next Green Zone plateau. Chaos is confusing and uncomfortable. But it eventually yields to the next step which is Order.

We put things into order in our own minds. We make sense of things. We learn what every part does and when it needs to be used. It becomes comfortable.

Time for me to insert some order about our subject of UP. I want you to think of a stoplight where red means stop. Yellow means proceed with caution and Green means go, go, go. This is how I think of life. There is a red zone, a yellow zone, and a green zone to every subject and every situation.

Absense, which we learned about in the last section, is a Red Zone occurrence. We are not even in the area. We might be able to see it from a distance, but we are not IN it. Presence is a Green Zone event, but it's green within a Red Zone situation of not knowing what needs to be known.

Chaos is in the Red Zone. The confusion keeps us from moving forward.

Order is in the Green Zone (again within a Red Zone of not knowing what we need to know. It is an oasis.)

See the pattern here? Red Zone, Green Zone, Red Zone, Green Zone. Every Red Zone can be transformed into a Green Zone and every Green Zone prepares us for the next Red Zone. In this way, we break the huge task of learning something new into smaller chunks that can be more easily assimilated.

By the time you finish this book, you should know which direction is UP and that will make you smarter than a lot of your peers and a lot more likely to succeed. In fact, having read this far puts you in better shape than many of the people around you. You have defined the Zones. Congratulations!

When I was a teenager, I learned to drive a car. It was a Volkswagon Bug which meant it was a simple car, but it had a stick shift. If you've never driven a stick shift you may wonder why I even mention it, but the stick shift requires a higher degree of coordination than an automatic. It has a clutch that has to be worked with the left foot while the right foot takes care of the brake and gas pedals. Your right hand is simultaneously occupied with moving the stick at precisely the right time to avoid stalling the car or damaging the transmission.

I practiced for many hours with no key in the car. Just moving the stick with the clutch engaged. That may be the reason my parents sold me the car for a mere $500. after I learned to drive it. They probably assumed I had damaged the transmission and who knows what else. Of course, $500. was some serious coin back then.

Back to the staircase. When you pull Order out of Chaos it feels great. That's what I did with identifying all the parts in that VW Bug. As I said, it's a simple car, so sorting it out was a lot easier than say, a jet, but it's not the difficulty of the step, it's about taking that step and not skipping over it. All learning involves ALL the steps every time. You may spend only a few seconds on a step or you may spend a few years. The bigger the project the more time some of the steps are going to need.

"How do I put order in when everywhere I look is Chaos?" you may ask and I'm glad you did. Pick something. Pick one thing and learn about it. Identify it. It doesn't matter what you pick. Just pick something and then another thing. Slowly it will begin to make sense and you will have created Order from Chaos.

Whenever you find yourself in Chaos, look around for one thing you can identify. Then another. Before you know it, you'll be out of the Chaos.

After my husband died, it took me months to get Present and put in some Order. In fact, it took at least a year. I neglected my thirteen-year-old and my business and my house and mySelf. But eventually, I did put in Order.

You're probably wondering how many steps we're talking about. We've only made it to Order and that seems like we're almost done. That's not the case, though. There are over fiteen steps to Mastery in any given area. Sixteen, to be exact. There are two parts to each step, the riser, and the landing. The riser is the red zone or yellow zone as you ascend. The landing is always the green zone.

"I don't want mastery, Linda. I just want to be able to do it well enough to get along."

That's fine. You don't have to follow the staircase all the way to mastery, but remember what I said about anger? Anger is at the top of the Red Zone. It's the last step before you break through to the Yellow Zone. But we are taught that anger is bad, so we shy away from it. This causes us to never be proficient in many, if any, subjects.

When we hit the Anger step we turn around and slide right back down, sometimes all the way to absence. We leave the subject completely and consider ourselves failures. How many times do you have to fail before you begin to believe you ARE a failure?

How many times will you need to win to believe you ARE a winner? Is it worth it? It has always been to me. I much prefer feeling like and being a winner.

So, let's look at the rest of the steps and see what it would take to get past Anger and move on to Stability or even Mastery. What comes after Order? Order is Green Zone, so we know the next step is a riser and so it's Red Zone. It's something we're going to have to learn, or conquer, right?

"I've failed over and over and over again in my life and that is why I succeed." Michael Jordan

Chapter 3

Sabotage and Trust

The next riser is Sabotage. How can that be a riser? Why would anyone sabotage? First let's look at the definition:

Sabotage

<u>noun</u>

sab·o·tage | \ ˈsa-bə-ˌtäzh \

Definition of *sabotage*

(Entry 1 of 2)

1 : destruction of an employer's property (such as tools or materials) or the hindering of manufacturing by discontented workers

2 : destructive or obstructive action carried on by a civilian or enemy agent to hinder a nation's war effort

3a : an act or process tending to hamper or hurt

b : deliberate subversion

sabotage

verb

sabotaged; sabotaging

transitive verb

: to practice sabotage on

    This makes it sound like Sabotage is always deliberate, but I can assure you, it is not. Sometimes, we Sabotage ourselves without ever knowing it was us much less why we did it.

Have you ever met someone who seems to be jinxed? They are constantly having bad things happen to them and around them. They can rarely hold a job. Their car insurance is more expensive than their car or car payment because they've had so many tickets or accidents or both. They just can't seem to do anything right. They can't win and Life never cuts them a break.

This is a perfect description of someone living in the Red Zone. And they are stuck at the stage of Sabotage. They had probably reached the next step, which is Trust, and slipped down into Sabotage. We look at them and hope they don't slip into absence.

No one likes to be in Sabotage, but it's one of the steps. If you know your way around the steps, up them and down them, then you can pass through many of the Red Zone steps quickly. So, it pays to study this material as much and as often as possible. Reading it once is good, but re-reading it is better.

When you're first starting out. Once a month would be a good plan.

Have you met people who don't write down instructions? They're sure they'll remember. That is another form of Self-Sabotage.

Just because you've turned Chaos into Order doesn't mean you're going to automatically remember where everything goes and what everything is called. But human nature whispers "You don't need to take notes. You got this."

Boom! You just received demerits for not completing a certain step of your job or for not putting tools back where they belong or for not calling everyone on the list to remind them of their appointments with the boss tomorrow. The potentials for Sabotage are endless.

I used to run a dental laboratory. We made teeth. There are a lot of steps to the process of making teeth and it is (or used to be) normal for a person to apprentice into the field. They would learn one step at a time and the whole learning process took approximately five years. At least, you had to have five years of experience in a lab before you could sit for the certification exam. Most people had to take the exam two or three times before they were certified.

So, at any given time you could be learning a new step from a more experienced technician and also be teaching a step to a new person. I remember a woman who was training a young man to make molds. Each time he started she would repeat the steps he would need to take. He finally said, "I KNOW how to do it. You don't have to tell me every time." So, the next time he had to do it, she did not tell him the steps. Boom! He forgot one step and ruined a half day's work for his teacher and almost got himself fired.

He had Sabotaged himself and his instructor. His instructor had Sabotaged herself. With the next step being Trust, you can imagine it took them a little while to graduate.

After you've wrestled with Sabotage for a few minutes or a few hours or a few days, you get to experience Trust. Trust is in a Green Zone bubble within a Red Zone area. Remember you're still putting Order into an area you didn't understand before. Don't fight the Chaos. Take each piece of information and organize it. Own it. If you keep at it, Chaos will always yield to Order. And Sabotage will always yield to Trust.

Any time you hit a Green Zone bubble, it's tempting to linger there. The Green Zone feels good. Things go right in the Green Zone. You don't even have to try. Things just fall into place. Who would want to leave?

But it's like living in a mansion located in a slum. Your house is nice, but wouldn't it be better to live in a nice neighborhood, too? As you learn more about the stairs you will find that every riser brings you closer to being in the Green Zone not as a bubble, but all the time. That is the goal.

So here you are at Trust. You trust yourself to do what you've learned and you've learned enough to be helpful. You trust yourself and your team trusts you. It's a nice feeling, but you haven't really mastered anything. You know how to do a small part without sabotaging anything. It's a win, but you must keep climbing the stairs if you want the truly big wins.

Some people reach Trust and just stop there. They never make enough money to buy a house in ANY neighborhood. Their paychecks are probably barely enough to keep an apartment paid for. But, they're comfortable. Trust is a comfortable place even if it is still in a Red Zone neighborhood.

Have you ever seen a video of someone learning to turn clay? They have a flat wheel in front of them and it's spinning. They put a lump of clay on the wheel and put their hand in the middle of it and it starts changing shape. A novice may learn to turn a cup without a handle and be very proud. S/he may turn it so well that s/he begins to trust her/himself with the clay.

S/he's ready to move to the next step. Being at Trust has become boring. S/he decides to move on to turning a vase. It isn't much more than turning a cup. It involves fluting the top and perhaps an indentation area in the middle.

S/he attempts it without help from the instructor. After all s/he can make a good cup. Why would s/he need help with the next logical step? S/he doesn't know what s/he doesn't know. S/he ends up destroying both the vase and the clay. Perhaps s/he needs help after all.

"A leader's job is not to do the work for others, it's to help others figure out how to do it themselves, to get things done, and to succeed beyond what they thought possible." Simon Sinek

Chapter 4

Destruction and Help

S/he has reached a riser called Destruction. "What makes this different from Sabotage?" you may ask. Good question. Sabotage sets you up for failure. Destruction IS failure. This is why we study. There are huge differences between some of the steps. And there are subtle differences between some of the steps. But, it's best not to skip any steps. And you don't want to start experiencing Destruction and think you have slipped back down into Sabotage, do you?

Of course not! It's always helpful to know exactly which step or riser you are on. You are now halfway to the Yellow Zone. That's an achievement. But the next few steps are difficult. These will be the steps that make you want to quit. These will be the steps that start to stir up anger and hostility.

Let's define Destruction.

destruction

<u>noun</u>

de·struc·tion | \ di-ˈstrək-shən

\

Definition of *destruction*

1 : the state or fact of being <u>destroyed</u> : <u>ruin</u> /scenes of death and destruction/ the destruction of their careers

2 : the action or process of destroying something /the destruction of the building

3 : a destroying agency /Alcohol will be his destruction.

Smash the vase and start over. Destroy the dead flowers you were trying to grow. Sand down the "not good enough" paint job. Try again, with help.

When I was apprenticing in a dental lab my mentor told me a story of a technician he had worked with years before. The fellow spent all morning setting up and waxing a set of dentures. They were beautiful. Nicest set of dentures my mentor (Walter Burnett) had ever seen. The proud young apprentice took the teeth to the department manager for approval before making a mold to make them out of acrylic.

The manager took them and admired them and showed them to several technicians. He said, "This is what premium dentures should look like." Then he threw them in his wax pot and melted them.

The apprentice was horrified. He had spent all morning on the case and the manager had said they were excellent. Why would he melt them?

"You haven't been paying attention," said the manager. "We don't charge for premium dentures.

We don't pay you to make premium dentures. We pay you to make fast dentures that fit and function. Now, go try again."

In his quest to make something perfect he forgot his goal, which was to make something acceptable and do it quickly. His manager destroyed his work that day but taught him a lesson he would never forget. Find out what is wanted and deliver THAT. He eventually quit that job to work for a smaller, but higher-priced (and higher-paying) laboratory. But that is another step further up the staircase and further along in his career.

So, sometimes you're the destroyer and sometimes you're the "destroyed." It might be as simple as ruining a batch of cookies and so, you completely destroy them as you scrape them into the trash bin. Destruction can feel good when you're frustrated, but don't mistake it for the Green Zone. Unless you are destroying something bad to replace it with something good, and even then, there's a fine line between good and bad when destruction is involved.

As you step up to the next Green Zone landing, you may be surprised that you are in the territory of Helpful. You may find that people are more helpful to you or you may find yourself being helpful to others. Maybe you want to help others climb out of the Red Zone.

In the example of the dental technician, he had learned a valuable lesson and was in a position to help others learn as well.

When I was a teenager, I had a paper route. Back in the 1960s, kids (over 12) would sell newspaper subscriptions to residents in their territory. Some people wanted delivery every day and others only wanted the paper on weekends. Some wanted only mornings and others wanted papers morning, afternoon, and weekends. "Paperboys" would fold and deliver the papers. I was the only girl "paperboy" in my district. I was teased a lot. But it was a step I'm glad I took. It instilled in me an entrepreneurial attitude that I cherish to this day.

I had two hundred potential customers in my territory, (an apartment building) but it was up to me to sell to them and collect the money, then pay for the papers I had used that week. I worked the route before school, after school, and early Saturday and Sunday. I started with two customers and built it up to about one hundred and fifty. My slow progress gave me time to learn what I was doing.

When I turned sixteen, my mother decided I needed a real job. So, I gave the paper route to my younger brother and went to work in a soda fountain at the local drug store.

As with any new job I had to go up the steps. I was around the levels of sabotage and destruction when two co-workers decided to Help (Green Zone). They pulled me aside one afternoon and said, "We like you. You're nice and easy to get along with. But the boss is talking about getting someone else because you're not fast enough, so we're going to show you how to go faster." And they proceeded to do just that. They were being Helpful and I was learning to be Helpful.

It was another Green Zone bubble. I was a Helper. I would wash glasses (really fast) and prep the sandwich trays, and get people their water and other helpful things. I would have one or two customers of my own, but the other girls would give me a small share of their tips in exchange for my help. Everyone was happy.

The day came when I was given an equal share of seats. (It was a counter soda fountain/grill.) I panicked. I had moved into the next riser of Red Zone. It's called Immobility.

"Some days it is a heroic act just to refuse the paralysis of fear and straighten up and step into another day." Edward Albert

Chapter 5

Immobility and Game Planning

immobile

adjective

im·mo·bile | \ (ˌ)i(m)-ˈmō-bəl

, -ˌbī(-ə)l also -ˌbēl \

1 : incapable of being moved : fixed

2 : not moving : <u>motionless</u> keep the patient immobile

Immobility is usually a result of being overwhelmed. You're not sure what to do so you do nothing. It's not something you can easily hide. It is a very difficult situation to get out of when you're in it.

It's easy to SAY, "Well just start moving." But when you're in Immobility, it's almost like being paralyzed. Which way should you move? How fast should you move? Maybe it's safer for everyone if you just stay still.

Now, that's the literal meaning of Immobility and we've all seen it happen to people in a crisis. They are not prepared. Maybe they thought they were, but now that the proverbial s#!t has hit the fan, they're stuck and consequently useless.

But there is another form of immobility. The kind that keeps you from taking the next step. The kind that holds you back from taking a class in something you've dreamed of doing. The Immobility that keeps you from calling about a job opening at

your favorite store or Mechanic or Dr's office, or
_____ (fill in the blank.)

Here you are just two steps from moving up to the Yellow Zone and you're stopped. Maybe you're afraid of messing it up or maybe you're afraid of doing it well, but recognize that YOU ARE STOPPED!

This is something you have to push through. Maybe you need a coach. If you can't afford one, you'll have to step up and be your own coach. Are your friends cheering you on? Or are they dragging you down? Telling you you're not ready. Telling you, you can't do it.

Real friends will always cheer you on. You are the average of the five people you spend the most time with. Maybe it's time to start looking for a friend who is higher up on the ladder. Someone who will coach you with honesty and a positive attitude.

I'm not saying shoot for the moon at this point. Having the richest most famous person on the planet as your best friend might be a stretch. But what about your manager? Or someone on your bowling team or league. People still bowl, don't they? Someone who is stable and friendly and enjoys their work will make a great cheerleader and when you've finished reading this book, so will you.

So, yes, force yourself to move. If it's at a diner & grill where you have customers waiting for their order. Or if it's in a hobby that you've been learning and gotten good enough to turn into a business or a paper route that's gotten big enough to need help to get it all done.

Immobility is not moving. So, MOVE! Get off of FaceBook or Instagram or whatever, and DO something to make YOU a better person. Find a meditation video on youTube and meditate for twenty minutes or even an hour. (Which is kind of not moving, but mentally it IS moving.)

You are never too young or too old, too high on the staircase of life or too low, to benefit from meditating every day. In fact, you may need it to get through your next Red Zone riser, which, by the way, is not a bubble. The Red Zone is always the real deal.

But we're getting ahead of ourselves. We don't want to skip the Green Zone bubble that comes after Immobile and that is Game Planning.

If you're going to move, it helps to have a plan and life is a series of Games when you get this high up the stairs so, it's a good idea to recognize the Game and plan it.

You can turn anything into a game. Laundry, grocery shopping, driving to work, work, cooking, reading a book, learning. It's all a game if you make it one, and isn't it more fun to play a game than drive to work?

Henry Ford was an innovator. In 1913 he developed the first moving assembly line. He wanted a way to make his cars more efficiently so they could be made less expensive. He succeeded, but there came a point where he thought they were stalled at a specific number of cars per shift. He knew they could produce more. And he was determined to produce a car that people could afford to buy.

As the night shift was arriving one night, he used a large piece of chalk and wrote a number on the pavement of the entry to the assembly line. It was big enough to be seen across the room and he drew a circle around it easily five feet across. He didn't say a word. It was the number to beat. The number of cars the day shift had produced that day. It was a challenge. It worked. The night shift sped up and produced more.

Ford had created a game for the workers to play. The two shifts began competing with each other. They began looking for new ways to tweak the assembly line to get the numbers up. Game Planning is a winning strategy. Most people love to play games. Human beings are quite competitive and don't forget: You can compete against yourself to reach a goal.

Look at the games we create to keep us alert when driving long distances. We will break the trip down into smaller destinations, making games out of spotting license plates, looking for landmarks, and more.

This Green Zone bubble is where you start identifying the things you want to make more fun. Actually, modeling the game or games comes later. For now, just look for the games and start planning to make them enjoyable. You're very close to breaking out   of   the   Red   Zone.

"If we could read the secret history of our enemies, we should find in each man's life, sorrow and suffering enough to disarm all hostility". Henry Wadsworth Longfellow

Chapter 6

Hostility and Modeling

It's time to look at Hostility and the dreaded ANGER. You wouldn't think of Games preceding Hostility, but what is a game without conflict which often precedes Hostility.

hostility

noun

hos·til·i·ty | \ hä-ˈsti-lə-tē

plural hostilities

deep-seated usually mutual <u>ill will</u> /glad to have gotten through the divorce proceedings without any visible signs of hostility /showed open hostility toward outsiders

b(1) : <u>hostile</u> action/ the Spanish expedition encountered hostility ... and was forced to flee— R. W. Murray

(2) hostilities plural : overt acts of warfare : <u>war</u> Peace talks were stalled after recent *hostilities*.

2 : conflict, opposition, or resistance in thought or principle /there was tension, there was hostility and envy in the air— Theodor Reik

Webster finds hostility to mostly be centered around war. Is it a coincidence then that many of the games we create are war games and usually competitive? Should we then skip games? Maybe eliminate them from the culture to keep hostility and anger to a minimum?

I, for one, don't think it would help. I think it would cause certain emotions to build up, that need, instead, to be released.

Games are an integral part of being human. Yes, games can lead to anger and even violence. Look at football, basketball, baseball, and hockey to name a few. Fights will sometimes erupt on the field. But they continue to be considered pleasurable pastimes. People enjoy games. Any activity treated as a game is automatically more fun.

But what do we do about the Hostility? We've been taught all our lives that anger is bad. Hostility is not acceptable. Social workers encourage us to experience "the emotion," but not to give in to violence. "Use your words." is a common expression.

Is it that simple? For some, it is, especially when they are operating in the Green Zone. But in the Red Zone Anger often leads to violence and someone "taking their ball and going home." Which, you may recall, is Absence. Or they may resort to violence which would be going down to destruction. What a quandary.

Giving up on a goal because it has made us angry is going absent. And this is where most people go absent from their ambitions. The going can get rough and they will stick it out. But if it makes them angry or frustrated, they will often leave never to return.

They feel like they have failed because they have. They have failed to push through the Hostility and reach the next Green Zone bubble, but more than that, they have fallen all the way down a chute. How many times can we do that before we begin to feel like a failure? All because we never learned that Anger is just another emotion to be experienced and moved on from. If you teach your kids one thing, teach them to be angry when they're angry. Feel it. Express it and move on.

The next Green Zone bubble is going to launch us into the Yellow Zone. The Yellow Zone is a place where people keep steady jobs, own houses, get married, and more. People in the Yellow Zone tend to work for other people which is miles better than working against other people like they do in the Red Zone.

People in the Yellow Zone have hope. They get lucky from time to time. It's very important to remember that we can be in all three zones at the same time. You might be in the Red Zone of learning some new software at work, but in the Yellow Zone at your actual job while ascending into the Green Zone in matters of spirituality.

There are a huge number of things that can be in different Zones like: communication, or effectiveness. How's your personal confidence level? Do you have empathy? What's your ability to take action? You have to look at your ethics and your ability to know. How is your sense of self? What is your Size of Games? Are you playing small to fit in? Do you have any power and how do you utilize it? These are only a few of the areas to look at and determine what zone you're in. But that is another book.

So, you can't look at the janitor and say, "S/he must be in the Red Zone." S/he may, in fact, be a Reiki

Master, or a talented artist, or a fabulous mother/father. There are forms that can determine where an individual is in the Zones across many areas of their life. There will be information in the back of this book about where you can contact someone to help you with that if you're interested. But don't think that because you read this book, you can judge what Zone people are in. It would be nice if it were that easy, but it isn't.

So, the last Green Zone bubble that sits in the Red Zone is Modeling and Standards.

I heard that. That collective, "WHAT?"

model

<u>noun</u>

mod·el | \ ˈmä-dᵊl

Definition of *model*

1 obsolete : a set of plans for a building

2 dialectal British : <u>copy</u>, <u>image</u>

3 : structural /design a home on the model of an old farmhouse

4 : a usually miniature representation of something/ a plastic model of the human heart also : a pattern of something to be made

5 : an example for imitation or emulation/ his written addresses are models of clearness, logical order, and style— A. B. Noble

6 : a person or thing that serves as a pattern for an artist especially : one who poses for an artist /His wife served as the model for many of his paintings.

7 : archetype

8 : one who is employed to display clothes or other merchandise /has appeared as a model in ads for swimsuits

9a : a type or design of clothing /girls, self-conscious in their Paris models— Paul Bowles

b : a type or design of product (such as a car) /offers eight new models for next year, including a completely restyled convertible

11 : a description or analogy used to help visualize something (such as an atom) that cannot be directly observed

12 : a system of <u>postulates</u>, data, and <u>inferences</u> presented as a mathematical description of an entity or state of affairs also : a computer simulation (see <u>simulation sense 3a</u>) based on such a system/ climate models

13 : <u>version sense 2</u> an experimental model of a bionic arm

<u>verb</u>

modeled or modelled; modeling or modelling\ 'mäd-liŋ , 'mä-dᵊl-iŋ

Definition of *model*

<u>transitive verb</u>

1 : to plan or form after a pattern : <u>shape</u> legislative institutions / primarily modeled on the English pattern

2 archaic : to make into an organization (such as an army, government, or parish)

3a : to shape or fashion in a plastic material /modeling figures from clay

b : to produce a representation or simulation (see <u>simulation sense 3a</u>) of using a computer to model a problem

4 : to construct or fashion in imitation of a particular model /modeled its constitution on that of the U.S.

5 : to display by wearing, using, or posing with modeled gowns

<u>intransitive verb</u>

1 : to design or imitate forms : make a pattern The students are modeling in clay.

2 : to work or act as a fashion or art model /Each contestant modeled in front of the judges.

model

<u>adjective</u>

Definition of *model*

1 : serving as or capable of serving as a pattern / a model student

2 : being a usually miniature representation of something/ a model airplane

Whew! That's a lot of definition. Modelling and Standards is an important subject. Games have to have models or avatars and rules. You have chosen the game. Now you must create the models and the standards or rules. It's best to find a Role Model. It's a key to reaching your goals.

Most of us default to our parents, or older siblings, or teachers as role models and that's fine while we're growing. But If you can choose a Role

Model, you can study that person. Read all about them. Get to know what makes them tick. Understand how they have succeeded.

First, they had to have a game. The game had to have players. They had to decide which player they wanted to be. Did they want to be the cop or the robber? Did they want to be the money magnate or the struggling pauper? Did they want to be the playright or the actor or the critic?

Who are the players in your favorite game? What standards will they be held to? What does the game board look like? Let's say you've decided to learn Real Estate. You have the primary players, the Realtors and Agents, but you also have the buyers and sellers. Without them, there's no game. You have Title companies and lawyers and bankers. You have inspectors and surveyors and architects. You have options! Pick one and get yourself a role model.

You also have standard operating procedures. It's up to you to learn who does what and which one you really want to be.

I know… People tell you to be yourself. But the truth is, you can create yourself as who you want to be. In order to have what you want to have, you need to do what needs to be done. And to do that, you have to be who you need to be. This is IMPORTANT! Be. Do. Have.

Can a ballerina be a lumberjack? Maybe, but it would be a lot easier for her to be a ballerina. If you want to have a family, you have to get married (in this society) and make children. To do that you have to be a good husband or wife. Obviously, you will need to be more than one thing, but if you know you need to be a good husband you can define that role and measure your progress in achieving it.

If you want to be an entrepreneur, what will that involve doing and having? If you want to sit around playing video games and eating pizza all day, you might want to scratch husband or wife off your list of things to be and scratch nice house and car off your list of things to have. But that's just my opinion and there are plenty of successful people in the Gaming industry.

This is where you decide what you want for the future. The good thing is you can always change your mind. Choose a new goal and a new avatar. Especially if you operate in the Green Zone.

"To establish true self-esteem we must concentrate on our successes and forget about the failures and the negatives in our lives." Denis Waitley

Chapter 7

Unestablished and Established

Time to celebrate. We're moving into the Yellow Zone! Where every other step is NOT Red Zone. Now we are moving from Yellow to Green at each new step. The Yellow Zone is filled with hope. Good things happen here.

We're still cautious. We're still critical. We work for other people or companies. This is probably where most people live. It's comfortable.

I've asked you not to try and place people in a zone. Then I sit here and tell you that most people are in the Yellow Zone. Am I a hypocrite? No, I'm just quoting statistics.

As we look at the steps in this zone, you will probably agree.

This is the time in the learning process when we begin to see the proverbial light at the end of the tunnel. We begin to realize that we CAN do this. We can learn to fly the jet. We may not be able to do it yet, but we will.

As we climb out of the Red Zone we move first through a step some call Disestablishment which means the taking apart of something already established. I think we also need to look at the word Unestablished. Let's look at the dictionary:

disestablish

<u>verb</u>

dis·es·tab·lish | \ ˌdis-ə-ˈstab-lish

disestablished; disestablishing; disestablishes

Definition of *disestablish*

transitive verb

: to deprive of an established status especially : to deprive of the status and privileges of an established church

And Unestablished

unestablished

adjective

un·es·tab·lished | \ ˌən-i-ˈsta-blisht

Definition of *unestablished*

: not established: such as

a : not firmly based/ an unestablished reputation /an unestablished business

b : having little or no previous success /unestablished writers

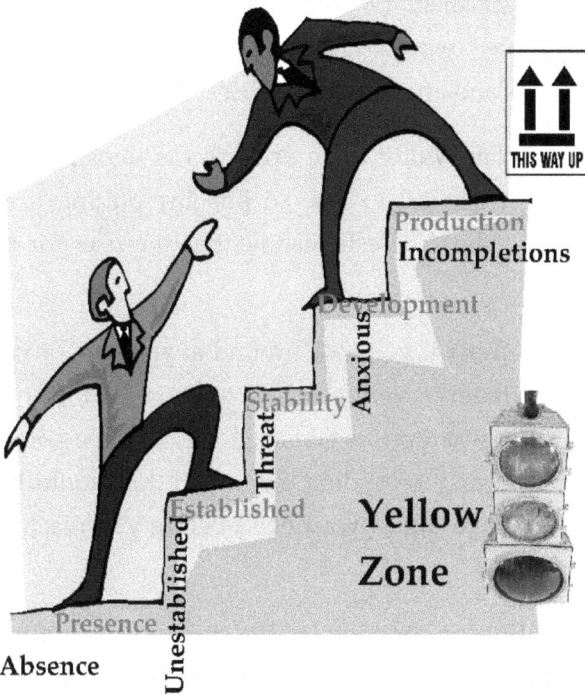

Finding UP

Green Zone

THIS WAY UP

Production
Incompletions

Development

Anxious

Stability

Threat

Established

Yellow
Zone

Unestablished

Presence

Absence

32 Steps to Mastery-13 through 20

Copyright 2019 Linda Anthony Hill

It seems to me that on the way up, the best word might be unestablished because we have not yet been established. On the way down, on the other hand, we would have previously established ourselves and are falling into disestablishment.

Alan Walter came up with the steps and he's no longer around to ask, so I'm just putting it out there. He chose Disestablishment as the riser for this step.

I think if you look around at your life or your job or whatever you're trying to learn and you see that what was once established seems to be coming apart, you may be sliding down and this would be a good place to dig in your heels before you reach the Red Zone.

But for climbing up the steps, I'm going with Unestablished. You have a game. You have players or avatars. You have rules, but you don't have much history. Your game is not yet established. It's time to put a little time in. Get some practice.

If you're learning a skill, you just keep doing what you're doing. See how much easier the Yellow Zone is? This riser, like all risers, is on the negative side of the steps and it's not anything that uncomfortable.

And it leads to the Green Zone step of Establishment! You have arrived. Not at your final destination, but certainly at **a** milestone. Of course, every step you take UP is a milestone to be celebrated.

There was a point with my dental lab when two of my employees were helping me tear a large piece of equipment apart to fix it. The rest of the crew (eight or so people) were continuing with their work and keeping things flowing. I suddenly felt a surge of pride. My company was established. It felt like it was a living breathing thing. And I had created it.

It didn't need me to keep it moving. My employees were capable of motivating themselves to get the work done. My little business was a real company. I cannot express how happy I was to be Established.

"You get a reputation for stability if you are stable for years." Mark Zuckerberg

Chapter 8

Threatened and Stable

No one will blame you for lingering in Establishment. It's a great place to be. Whether we're talking about a family or a job or a beehive. You have something now.

The downside to that is when you have something there may be others who see it and decide they want it. Maybe they think they can just take it from you and not have to put in the work you did.

That's right, you begin to feel Threatened. Sometimes (often) the perceived threat is imaginary. Sometimes it's real, but it doesn't really matter.

Feeling threatened is not good for you. It keeps you on edge. It makes you look over your shoulder when you should be looking UP.

But where is UP when you're threatened. Maybe someone doesn't like what you've done with the lawn at your new house. Maybe someone from the Red Zone will decide to tag your car. Maybe your work will slow down and they will have to lay you off.

There are so many things to feel threatened by. You're on shaky ground. You're established, but you're not stable yet.

Shortly after I felt that my lab was established, my landlord doubled my rent. I wasn't imagining a threat. This was a huge threat from where I least expected it.

I had worried about having so many employees and losing a big customer. That was always a threat. Or what if with all this work, one of my employees quit. How would we keep up? But having my rent doubled? I hadn't anticipated that one.

My accountant convinced me that I needed to buy my own building. That way no one could ever raise my rent again. It didn't take much convincing. Instead of pouring my money down the pockets of my landlord, I could, in essence, put that money in my own pocket. After paying back the loan, of course.

Owning my own building pushed me up to Stability. It also sparked the next Yellow Zone event, but we know to expect that, don't we?

Here's the thing, when things start going wrong, it's good to be able to look at a list or chart and determine where you are. Once you know where you are, you can choose to stop falling and either bounce over to the positive (Green) step or up to the next higher negative step or even down to the next lower Green step. The important thing is to stop sliding down. Grab a foothold on a Green landing and hang on.

Now, from Threatened the next step is Green so it's positive. It's called Stability. When you start feeling stable, you're less likely to feel Threatened. You've got your footing.

When I started writing books I went through these same steps. It took winning an award for my first novel to feel established, but I still wasn't stable. I doubted my own ability to "do it again." I had to publish two more books before I felt like I was firmly in Stability.

stability

noun

sta·bil·i·ty | \ stə-ˈbi-lə-tē

plural stabilities

Definition of *stability*

1 : the quality, state, or degree of being stable: such as

a : the strength to stand or endure : firmness

b **:** the property of a body that causes it when disturbed from a condition of equilibrium or steady motion to develop forces or moments that restore the original condition

c **:** resistance to chemical change or to physical disintegration

2 **:** residence for life in one monastery

So, stability is like a firm foundation from which to grow. It is a Green Zone bubble in a Yellow Zone neighborhood. It's a stage you can feel good about and many people choose to stop there.

You will find as you rise up the ladder that certain steps have negative aspects you can live with, like Threatened. It's not great, but if you have to have a negative nudge, you could do worse. Just look at all the negatives in the Red Zone. Yes, the Yellow Zone is a place where many people choose to spend their entire lives. But, if you were willing to settle, you wouldn't have picked up this book. From stability we reach into Anxiety.

"If I knew what I was so anxious about, I wouldn't be so anxious." Mignon McLaughlin

Chapter 9

Anxious and Development

Most of us are familiar with Anxiety. At this point, I'm going to interject an opinion, a Public Service Announcement, if you will. When you are learning something new like training for a new job or learning to parachute out of a plane or just how to bake cookies, there is a time when you will experience anxiety and sometimes depression. It's one of the steps. It's part of working the formula. Expect it.

But some people have something called clinical anxiety or clinical depression. These people experience anxiety and/ or depression when they are not on the appropriate steps. This is when a person should think about discussing it with their doctor. Not for occasional bouts, but for sustained Anxiety or depression, do yourself a favor and make an appointment. There is such a thing as a chemical imbalance which requires treatment.

clinical depression

noun

Definition of *clinical depression*

: depression that is a medical condition *Clinical depression* is more serious than the occasional bouts of sadness that most people deal with.

When you experience Anxiety or Depression, look at the steps and ask yourself, "Is this part of the Finding UP formula? Have I been working in the area of this emotion I'm feeling?"

If the answer is yes, keep working the formula and you will come out on the next landing. If the answer is no, consider that you may be experiencing something that requires a doctor.

I know. Most self-help teachers advocate meditation (as do I) and affirmations and what have you, but we have a formula and if your "symptoms" do not line up with the formula, and the situation has been ongoing for you, it's worth asking for medical help. You may not need it. But what if you do? You could save yourself a lot of frustration. End of PSA.

Back to Anxious. It is not a comfortable place to be, yet much of society chooses to live there. Is it a choice? I think so. One could just as easily move on up to Development. But fear keeps us at Stability. So, there is always Anxiety and Threatened lurking to the side waiting to draw us back into the Yellow Zone.

This is where skills are Developed and honed. This is where we get really good at what we've chosen to learn. It's a time of doing the same thing again and again and improving each time we do it. Success here is measurable.

We're starting all kinds of projects to learn even newer skills and use the skills we've recently acquired. And we're approaching the Green Zone, that magical place where we are usually in the right place at the right time for splendid opportunities of all kinds.

Life is good. Except for the occasional Anxiety and the ever-growing list of Incomplete projects.

"Being busy does not always mean real work. The object of all work is production or accomplishment and to either of these ends there must be forethought, system, planning, intelligence, and honest purpose, as well as perspiration. Seeming to do is not doing." Thomas A. Edison

Chapter 10

Incompletions and Production

So many projects, so little time. It's easy to spot this riser by the number of unfinished projects you have. You have become a master at starting things. You just can't seem to find the time or inclination to move forward on any of them. So, you start another one.

When I worked in the dental lab I was surrounded by incompletions. I came up with a To-Do list of steps to be completed on each case, each day. It was the only way for me to stay Productive. Otherwise I would become overwhelmed with the number of incompletions all around me and drop all the way down into the Red zone at immobile.

Remember the Red Zone where you're usually in the wrong place at the wrong time? Without my To-Do list the day fell apart quickly and by the end of the day I would look around and realize that I was going to have to stay late to play catch up.

When you find yourself in the midst of too many incompletes in your life there's a tool to help get back to Production.

First: Make a list of every project that you have started. This needs to be a real list, not a mental list. You should include everything from the book you're currently reading to the deck you started building last Spring, to the soap-making project, to planning the trip you're taking for vacation, to the online class you started to_____ (fill in the blank.) Put down everything you can think of.

Now prioritize them by importance. Number them. Highest priority is number one etc. Now rewrite the list. Take number one on the list and break it down into smaller steps if possible. Obviously, the step of putting the ladder back in the garage doesn't require a breakdown, but finishing the deck you started last Spring does. Don't worry about the rest of the projects for now. Put your attention on job number one. As you complete a step, check it off the list. As you complete a project check it off the list and write a list for the next project.

This puts you in the Green Zone step of Production. You are now producing results. AND you are at the top of the Yellow Zone! You are now as big as your problems. They are the same problems you faced in the Red Zone, but they seem much smaller now because YOU have gotten bigger. You can handle them more easily now.

This step is all about production. Use it to finish things and make room on your schedule for bigger and better things.

Of course, there's a Yellow Zone step waiting for you.

"Success is not final: Failure is not fatal. It is the courage to continue that counts." Winston Churchill

Chapter 11

Reluctance and Success Breakout

Welcome to the bottom of the Green Zone. Granted, this step is a Yellow Zone bubble in the Green Zone, but You're here! Congratulations!

If you look Reluctance up in Merriam-Webster, it will tell you that it's the act of being reluctant. So, here's the definition of Reluctant.

Reluctant

adjective

re·luc·tant | \ ri-ˈlək-tənt

Definition of *reluctant*

: feeling or showing aversion, hesitation, or unwillingness/
reluctant to get involved also : having or assuming a specified
role unwillingly/ a reluctant hero

Some people are reluctant to be successful.
Some are reluctant to try because they fear failure.
This step is about dealing with success. Can you
handle it? Do you resist it? Can you define it?

Merriam-Webster can.

success

noun

suc·cess | \ sək-ˈses

Definition of *success*

1a : degree or measure of <u>succeeding</u>

b : favorable or desired outcome also : the attainment of wealth, favor, or <u>eminence</u>

2 : one that <u>succeeds</u>

3 obsolete : <u>outcome</u>, <u>result</u>

So, this step finds you Reluctant to take the next Green Zone step into Success. That feeling may last a few seconds or a few years or any point in between the two. What determines that? Lots of things. Mostly, though, it's how much emotional baggage you're lugging around with you. There have been many books written about how to get rid of the baggage. I'll list some in the back of the book.

This book is about finding which emotional anchors are holding you down right now. Most of us have anchors on every step and every emotion a human is capable of feeling, but if you're in the Red Zone at Sabotage it's not going to be a big help to get rid of the anchor on anxiety. You need to find the one that deals with Sabotage.

There are a lot more tools than are contained in this book. This is a starting point. A list. A roadmap. You will run into detours. Keep the map handy, so you know what your next step should be. (This book. This book is the map.)

The trouble with baggage is that it's virtually invisible to the one carrying it. (not in real life, of course.) Sometimes you need help to see it. That is what talk therapy is for. If you can't afford therapy, that's what friends are for. A **good** friend will tell you when you are blowing a good opportunity for success. They'll also help you see that that pyramid scheme is NOT a good opportunity for success, but a franchise might be.

Make sure the friend you listen to is NOT residing in the Red Zone. Are they pretty lucky? Do they seem to magically be at the right place at the right time a lot? Do they have a positive attitude about life and the everyday setbacks that pop up sometimes? Do they believe that people are basically good?

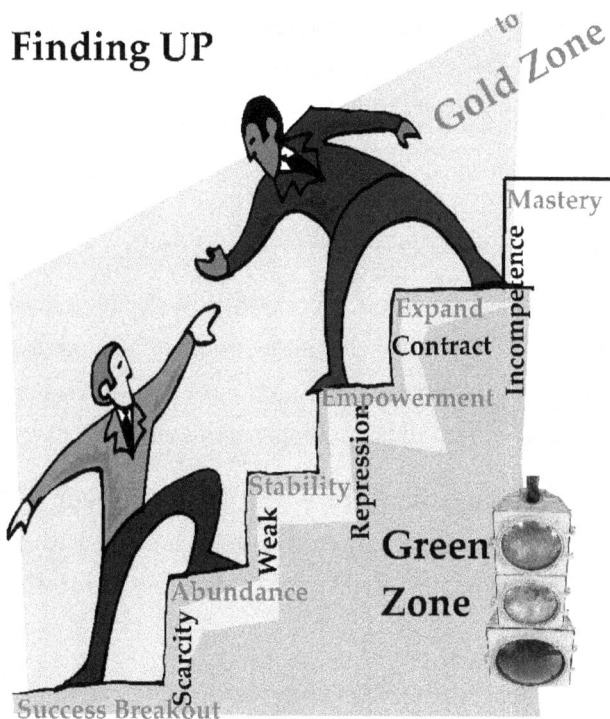

Finding UP

to Gold Zone

Mastery

Incompetence

Expand
Contract

Empowerment

Repression

Stability

Weak

Green Zone

Abundance

Scarcity

Success Breakout

Reluctance

32 Steps to Mastery-21 through 32

81

Are you ready for a Success Breakout? It's time.

What is a Success Breakout? You've been holding yourself back for a long time. Or a few seconds depending, again, on your baggage. Let's refer to the baggage as anchors. Things, mostly emotions, that trigger downward motion.

So, when you breakout, you get bigger. Not physically. The YOU that some people call a soul. The real YOU. When you're bigger you can move faster, float higher and flick problems aside with one finger.

This is the point where you own your YOU. You take responsibility for the good and the bad. You get out of your own way and allow yourself to succeed.

Did you think you were going to find UP without touching a little on the woo-woo? Add the movie "What the BLEEP Do We Know" to your list of things to study. It will take you down the Quantum Physics rabbit hole. We're not going there today, though.

Let's just leave it at: You're going to feel bigger than Life.

"Many a man curses the rain that falls upon his head, and knows not that it brings abundance to drive away the hunger." Saint Basil

Chapter 12

Scarcity and Abundance

From the high of Success Breakout you're going to run into the concept of Scarcity in the midst of Abundance.

In the Red Zone you were really in scarcity. Now you're in the Green Zone. This is the land of

Abundance. There is no Scarcity of anything here. So, why are you in a Yellow Zone bubble of Scarcity?

Many of us are indoctrinated into the rule of scarcity from an early age. We grow up thinking that the supply of any given item is limited. Whether it's candy or gold or money or love, we operate under the assumption that there's not enough to go around. We couldn't be further from the truth.

This universe has an abundance of everything. Remember the Doritos commercial? Eat all you want. We'll make more. It's true. Whatever you desire exists in abundance and if we run out, we'll just make more.

When I quit smoking, I made a point of not smoking my last few cigarettes. I still have them in the bottom of a purse in the closet. My reasoning was that craving is at its peak when we have smoked our last cigarette. I have left the house to get smokes at three in the morning rather than wake up with none. I was completely addicted to cigarettes, both physically and psychologically.

With three or four in my bag, I'm in abundance and so don't need to smoke one right now. Sounds crazy, but it helped. I've been nicotine free since 2001. I can sit in a smoke-filled room and never crave one. (But that's another book.)

Scarcity is a scary thing. Here you've just gone through Success Breakout and you're looking down the barrel of Scarcity. There won't be enough clients. There isn't enough money. There won't be enough workers. The trouble is that Scarcity is self-fulfilling. The more you focus on it, the more you will see it, and eventually experience it. Even though we know the universe is self-replenishing.

There was a time when my budget consistently came up short by about twenty dollars a paycheck. Now twenty dollars is not a lot of money, but short is short. And short is Scarcity. I moved the figures around and cut out everything I thought I could live without, but I was still short every two weeks. Consequently, my credit card debt grew each month. This only added to the feelings of Scarcity.

Then one day I listened to a motivational tape. (We had cassettes back then.) It said in a very powerful way that if you don't have enough money you need to quit trying to make do with less. Make more money! Make yourself more valuable to your employer or get a second job or turn your hobby into income. Find a way to make more money.

You're not going to believe this, but that idea had not occurred to me. I was operating from Scarcity. In my mind, at that point in time, there was no more money to be had. I needed to shrink my needs.

That motivational tape had a huge impact on me. I found a job as a lab manager which paid more and had better benefits and I pushed my husband (now deceased) to look for a better job and he found it.

We had flipped ourselves from Scarcity to Abundance

These two steps are very similar to Expansion and Contraction which are further up the ladder. But you don't have to Contract to face Scarcity and you don't have to Expand to find Abundance. The Green Zone is where you start experiencing the woo-woo. Thoughts become reality and desires can often be granted instantly. Take all you want. The universe will create more.

You may want to stay in Abundance for a long while. Some will stop here, but that puts them ever on the cusp with Scarcity. Try to remember that Abundance is always there. Wherever you are on the ladder, Abundance is available. You only have to look for it. Attitude is everything in the Green Zone. And there's a Green Zone bubble at the very bottom of the staircase at Presence.

The next step is surprising. At least it was to me. I would expect this Yellow Zone bubble to be in the Red Zone. But here it is in the middle of the Green Zone. It's called Weakness.

"Pessimism leads to weakness, optimism to power." William James

Chapter 13

Weakness and Power

One doesn't expect to find weakness in the Green Zone. I didn't anyway. Weakness has always been taboo in my family. It just wasn't tolerated. Which may have caused a type of weakness. Feeling weak sparks a shutdown for me. I don't want anyone to see it, so I close myself off from prying eyes. I can't think of anyone who wants to show their weakness.

But here I go. My biggest weakness is probably health. When I was younger, I had a lot of health problems. I would miss school for days at a time. I've had my fair share of surgeries, too. The older I get, the healthier I seem to get. But it was a big issue for the first thirty or forty years.

Knowing what your Weaknesses are is a good defense. It's an area of life that's often hard to look at.

Let's go back to learning to drive. In the Green Zone of driving one might be thinking of doing it professionally, either as someone's driver or as a race car driver, or as a mechanic or designing cars. This is the point in the process where your Weakness will show up. Maybe having passengers is a Weakness or maybe hairpin turns cause you trouble. Maybe you don't like to come to a full stop. Maybe you have a hard time driving in the rain.

The riser between Abundance and Power is where any weaknesses will present themselves. You can choose to confront and amend those areas or you can choose to ignore them. If you choose the latter, it will bite you in the future.

The time to deal with Weakness is when it presents itself. Whatever your Weakness is, work on it.

My true Weakness is math. I have numerical dyslexia. It has cost me a lot of money over the course of my life. Knowing that, my first employee was a bookkeeper. I made the numbers their job. That made me less Weak, but not invulnerable. I still had to understand what her figures meant.

There were spreadsheets to be read and multiple reports. I didn't have to generate those reports, but I had to be able to read them. Knowing the bottom line is helpful, but knowing how you got to the bottom line so you can tweak things is vital.

Now, I'm a writer. Do I need math for that? You bet. I have to analyze data to know which ads are working and which ads are just costing money. There is a science to it and it's based on math. So, once again life has thrown up my Weakness to be dealt with. How should I handle it? I'll probably take a class. In fact, I'm taking one now that's underscoring the need for algebraic formulas to sell books.

As we deal with and get rid of Weakness in an area, we step into our Power. This is an almost intoxicating step. Power can make you dizzy. It's very heady stuff. As in, it can go to your head.

What we do with Power says a lot about us. I've been reading a lot lately about very Powerful people who are using that Power to help people get an education or get their health under control or learn to be self-sufficient. They are probably going to zoom past the next Yellow Zone bubble. And they're doing it all fairly privately.

They are not looking to build their Power from helping others overcome their weaknesses. They're just looking to help. Of course, good PR never hurts. Especially if you want to run for office some day.

Most of us never know that kind of Power. We feel good to have Power over our own circumstances. If your goal is to have a happy healthy family, that is no less important than being the mayor of a city, but it is less powerful. Remember lofty goals require far more Power. There are considerably less people in positions of Power. If you are striving for Mastery, you must obtain some kind of Power. And you must learn to use it wisely or you will end up in another Yellow Zone bubble called Repression.

"It is easier to pull someone up than to push them up." Isaac Newton

Chapter 14

Repression and Empowerment

Repression is a two-edged sword. You can repress others or you can repress yourself. Why would you want to do either? Let's look at repressing others. Some people in Power do exactly that. They use their Power to Repress anyone below them on the stairs. They look at Power as a weapon to be used against others. Which is what makes this a Yellow Zone, and some would say a Red Zone, bubble.

When a person works against, they are acting in the Red Zone. When a person works FOR, they are acting in the Yellow Zone. When a person works WITH, they are acting in the Green Zone. A city manager who works with the citizens of the city to create beautiful parks and city venues is in the Green Zone. That city will prosper.

If a city manager tries to Repress the citizens by working against them and their efforts to improve the city, that manager, and consequently that city, is operating in the Yellow to Red Zone. Their future is not very bright.

Yes, knowing the Zones can help you predict the future.

The best way to predict the future is to create it the way you want it by finding people who want the same future you do and working WITH them to accomplish your combined vision. That is not Repression. It's Empowerment.

When you Empower others, beautiful things happen.

But I'm getting ahead of myself. We talked about repressing others and why one would want to

96

do it. What about Repressing one's self? Why would anyone do that?

If I use my Power to hurt others, my conscience might take over and begin to Repress my own Power. That's one reason. Can you think of more? If I use my own Power to enslave others or starve others or in any way Repress or harm others, my innate goodness will take over and cause me to Repress my own Power.

This is my belief and you don't have to share it, but I have to, at least, share it with you. I believe that no matter where you are on the ladder, you have a good heart. Yes, I believe even Hitler started with a measure of good. And this is where you ask, "What about Hitler? He had extreme Power. How could someone so cruel climb this ladder into the High Green Zone and still seem so Red Zone?"

Remember back in the beginning of this book when I told you that you can be in multiple places on the stairs at the same time and different parts of your life can even be on different staircases? Certain areas may be Green, while other areas may be Red. Einstein probably couldn't have crafted a chair or a clock. He had not spent his life Mastering those things. He was most likely Red Zone in those areas. Instead he Mastered Physics.

Hitler did not fully Master World Domination, but he gave it a good try. He neglected his positive assets to a degree and ascended the negative aspects of the stairs. He had Weaknesses that prevented him from seeing what he was doing to the world.

But I don't believe he was inherently bad. I believe we're all inherently good. But life gives us a body that doesn't work correctly or a brain that is chemically imbalanced. It throws horrible experiences at us that shape us in ways we can't even imagine.

He is responsible for his actions, but we don't know what conditions life threw at him to make him seem so heartless. He fully believed he was saving the world.

And eventually, before gaining absolute Mastery, life knocked him down so far that he committed the ultimate act of Absence, suicide.

We can be our own worst enemies. But when we Empower others we reach down and help them ascend the steps. Instead of Repressing, we Empower.

We give others responsibility and let them be the best people they can be. In turn they lift us up. This is UP. We have not reached Mastery, but we are definitely in the right territory. If you feel you're in the Green Zone, but not big enough to empower anyone, you might want to take a look at the size of games you're playing.

If you have a small business with one employee, you can be in the Green Zone and empowering one person. If you're in the Green Zone and Vice President of Communications in a large corporation, you're playing a bigger game while still being in the Green Zone. You have the opportunity to empower hundreds of people.

Of course, there are other ways to Empower people. Take reading. All the same steps. What would Empowerment look like in reading? Maybe it's teaching others to read. Or teaching others to teach others. Maybe it would involve reading to the blind, though that seems more like Helpful, which is a Green Zone bubble. The important thing is to get into the Green Zone from wherever you are. Any Green Zone gets you back on a positive landing. Positive landings are where you'll find your Power.

Always look for a Positive Green Zone step or bubble. Use it to get your footing and proceed UP.

That said, the next step is, of course, Yellow. How do you feel about Contraction?

"It is a sign of contraction of the mind when it is content, or of weariness. A spirited mind never stops within itself; it is always aspiring and going beyond its strength." Michel de Montaigne

Chapter 15

Contraction and Expansion

Contraction is simply getting smaller. Playing smaller games. Having smaller wins. It probably is triggered by a big loss. Losing a mate. Losing a parent. Losing a game. These are all reasons for a person to go from Empowerment to Contraction.

We all sympathize with the widow who has lost their mate. We give them time and space to recover. But we might serve them better if we make sure that they don't make themselves smaller.

The person who is getting smaller needs to deal with the emotions driving them down. Those emotions must be fully experienced lest they become anchors weighing the person down.

Contraction is a step that can't be rushed. It takes as long as it takes. It might be quick, but it could be long. There's no speeding up the grieving process over losing a loved one or losing a company that you built from scratch. Losing the paper route... For me, Contraction is usually caused by loss. For you it may be something different.

We are each unique. Our triggers are ours alone. Our anchors are the same way. There are questions you can ask yourself to determine your unique triggers and anchors. Here's a good one: What were you doing right before you dropped out of the Green Zone? What happened?

It's unique to you because it happened to you. No one else can answer the questions for you. This is not the time to call in a psychic. Dig deep. Find your answers. Over time you may notice a pattern. Every time things are going right (Green Zone) something happens to pull me back down. What do all the "somethings" have in common?

There's a story of a fisherman in New England. A couple was walking the beach when they came upon a fisherman with a bucket of crabs he was using as bait. "Why don't you have a cover on the bucket?" the woman asked. "Aren't you concerned about them getting out? They can reach the top by crawling on each other."

"No," said the fisherman. "If there was only one crab in the bucket, it might be able to crawl out, but crabs will pull each other back in. As long as you have two or more crabs in there, you don't have to be concerned. They won't let each other escape."

It had certainly given the woman something to think about. You see people are a lot like crabs sometimes. The further down the Zones they are, the more they will try to pull their companions back down as they begin to rise up the staircase.

What does this have to do with Contraction and Expansion? Your friends, though they wish you well, don't usually want you to Expand. They will do little things to cause you to contract. They don't want to lose you and they don't know what you now know. They're content to be where they are and for you to be there with them.

Am I suggesting that you end your friendships? No. But be vigilant that your friends aren't sub-consciously holding you back, keeping you contracted. Get them their own copy of this book and give them a hand up instead of letting them pull you down. Your Expansion is vital. You are almost at Mastery.

"She who succeeds in gaining the mastery of the bicycle will gain the mastery of life." Susan B. Anthony

Chapter 16

Incompetence and Mastery

You already know that there is a Yellow Zone bubble between you and Mastery. It's called Incompetence. How can someone be so close to Mastery and still be Incompetent?

That's all that's left to tackle. Any areas of Incompetence will show up when you are on the verge of Mastery.

They will probably show up when you least need them. Did you get by driving all this time and never need to parallel park? You'll have to now. And it'll probably be in front of everyone that matters to you.

Did you think you had Mastered walking which implicitly includes running and dancing? It might be time to show off your Texas Two Step skills or lack thereof. I'm sure you see the pattern here. Mastery is your next goal, so you will be confronted with every aspect of whatever you're learning or ascending that you haven't yet mastered. Especially the things you skipped over. It's time to go back and prove to yourself, or to the world that you can, in fact, filet a fish.

You didn't know that was part of Mastering fishing? Always remember, you don't know what you don't know.

That's why Incompetence can be such a difficult step. There can be things you haven't learned simply because you didn't know about them.

While writing this book, I've also been taking a class on effectively using Amazon Advertising for authors. I started at absence because I had tried using Amazon ads and failed miserably, so I went Absent. Totally Red Zone where online advertising in general was concerned.

I've risen to the Yellow Zone of Incompletions. There are lessons still to be learned. There are assignments I didn't do for one reason or another. The point is, I know where I am and what my next step is. But I also know that ultimately, I will face the things I skipped over because I was incompetent in the area. That's if I plan to take this to Mastery.

There's a lot to be said for being anywhere in the Green Zone. You don't have to take every skill to Mastery. Maybe you don't want to be a race car driver. You just want to be able to get around without being in an accident. That's okay. But I highly advise at least taking everything you attempt into the Green Zone.

Life is just easier in the Green Zone. Problems seem so much smaller in the Green Zone. I'll include a graphic that shows that your problems don't get bigger as you descend into the Red Zone. YOU get smaller. The opposite is also true. The same problem that seemed bigger than life in the Red Zone is a mere pebble to be flicked aside when you are in the Green Zone. All problems seem smaller in the Green Zone, even though you will encounter much larger problems here.

In the Red Zone a two-hundred-dollar problem could be the difference between eating or paying the rent.

In the Yellow Zone it may take a two-thousand-dollar problem to seem bigger than you. In the Green Zone, it may require a twenty-thousand-dollar problem to look as big as you are. It's all relative. But the more Green Zone skills you have in your

arsenal, the better life in general gets. It may take years, but take something to Mastery. And know that when you feel Incompetent, you may be close to Mastery.

The trick is to be able to move up and down those steps easily. Allow yourself to be in Chaos in an area, while remaining in Production or even Success Breakout or higher in others.

YOU in the Green Zone
Your Green Zone Problems

YOU in the Yellow Zone
Your Yellow Zone Problems

YOU in the Red Zone
Your Red Zone Problems

My best advice I can give you is to Master something. Make it something you can be proud of.

Learn to dance. Or learn to do Judo or Paint or any number of things that teach you in gradients starting at Presence. You will find that a good teacher or mentor will take you through most, if not all, of the steps in this book.

Mastery is funny because you technically "master" each step of the subject on the way to Mastery **OF** the subject. When you have mastered a step, you can then teach it to someone else. In fact, teaching a step is a great way of owning that skill.

Any skill you can teach should be a source of great pride. You know the saying, "Those who can, do. Those who can't, teach?" Well, it's total Bu!!S**t. Those who can't, certainly don't teach.

I'll never forget when I was in second grade. I hadn't mastered much, but I could read a second-grade book. My teacher and the first-grade teacher decided to try something. They paired each first grader with a second grader and let us find a spot on the schoolgrounds to read. The first grader would read a first-grade book to the second-grader.

111

I don't know what the first graders got out of it, but I was so proud to be able to do this step. It has stuck with me for sixty years. In my mind I was helping teach someone who was one step lower on the staircase. Not that I understood the Zone concept back then, but I understood grades and gradients well enough.

So, Mastery is a place where things go so right it borders on magic. Being in the right place at the right time is only one of the advantages.

When athletes talk about being in the Zone, they describe the ball seeming huge and unmissable. They talk about time seeming to slow down so that they can make the shot. They're describing the top of the Green Zone. And the same things happen to people in business and the arts and more. Mastery has its perks. Incompetence is just a bump in the road to Mastery. Until it's more…

If you're not prepared for it, Incompetence can make you slide down those steps like you were playing Chutes and Ladders.

Mastery is like Guru status. Imagine how hard Incompetence can hit you when you are so close to being a Guru. It seems almost impossible that someone with so much skill and knowledge could be incompetent at anything.

It brings to mind FDR, Franklin Delano Roosevelt, thirty second president of the U.S.A. He had reached a level of Mastery that few have. The leader of the most powerful country in the world. He was the definition of the top of the Green Zone.

He could communicate with anyone about anything. He loved life and always looked for the good in people and events. He was able to take action without reservations. He delivered what he promised. He was confident and sure of himself while being willing to be at risk. He had big dreams and he was an achiever.

Then he became ill. Eventually, he could no longer walk. Can you imagine becoming incompetent at walking? But he was still a Master at leadership. He lost none of the traits listed above.

The staircase is always a dance between the negative risers of the staircase, the going up or coming down and the positive side, the landing step. It's always safer to have both feet on the landings, but you can't rise up without taking one foot off.

What comes after the Green Zone, you may ask, and I'm so glad you did. When we have reached Mastery our next step up is into something we like to call the Gold Zone. This is the place of miracles and magic.

"I think all of us create our own miracles."
Michael Landon

Chapter 17

The Gold Zone

Miracles and Magic

This is the area where dreams come true. Here you can think of wanting something and it will appear. Some of us get to see this Zone briefly from time to time and write it off as a coincidence. Some people I know spend months at a time in the Gold Zone.

A few years ago, I was in a particularly high Green Zone level of living and I decided one day that

I wanted a personal filing cabinet that looked like an antique and would fit in the family room without looking like a klunky file cabinet.

Now at the time we lived in a small town with no more shopping than a Walmart, an Albertson's, and a Dollar General. It was before Amazon so…we shopped a lot at the Walmart.

As it happened, we went to the Walmart the day after I decided I wanted this piece of furniture, not a stock item at any Walmart I've ever seen. We walked in the front door and there it was. They had it on display at the entry to the store. There was no way I could miss it. And wouldn't you know it? It was the right color of wood and the price was very reasonable.

This was not plastic or paper veneer either. It was a beautiful, elegant piece of wood furniture completely assembled. We bought it on the spot.

The next day they were sold out and I have never seen such a cabinet in a Walmart since.

Coincidence? I don't believe in coincidences, do you? I thought it and it was made available.

That wasn't the only time. My husband and I had a rental property that needed a mini-fridge. Not one of those dorm refrigerators that can also be used as a microwave table and have only one door either. We needed it to look like a conventional refrigerator only smaller.

Once again, we walked into Walmart and there it was. On display in the entry area. The price was good, but we hesitated. We said we'd come back for it another day. Never saw it or anything like it at the store again. When life offers you what you asked for, don't walk away. Say Thank You, and take it home with you right then and there.

I have other similar stories, but you get the idea. Life in the Gold Zone is magical. Take something to Mastery and find out for yourself.

One of my mentors, Alan Walter had some great stories about life in the Gold Zone. I highly recommend you read his books, especially The

Secrets book. It doesn't talk about the Zones much, but it talks about the things that can cause you to get stuck on a step.

There are the big things, naturally. Like divorce, death of a loved one, losing a job, and so many more. All these things can leave marks on you. Triggers that will get in your way as you move up the steps. Thoughts that will stop you from following through. Hidden thoughts that will cause Self Sabotage.

The Secrets to Increasing Your Power, Wealth, and Happiness addresses many of these triggers and how to erase their negative effects on you. It's worth reading over and over again. I may have already mentioned this, but it's worth mentioning over and over again, too.

You can also call the good folks at ACLC.com (Advanced Coaching and Leadership Center) to get some coaching and courses on a host of subjects including the Zones. Ceil is a good friend and will point you in all the right directions.

There's also Catherine Taylor in Australia. She's a personal coach worth listening to and also a good friend. Find her on Facebook at https://www.facebook.com/CatherineTaylorPowerho use/

Back to the Gold Zone... I've only touched on it because I've only touched on experiencing it. It's a bit like being King Midas though, from what I've heard.

You'll notice that I haven't given you any of the steps, positive or negative, for the Gold Zone. The steps in that Zone aren't very well marked out. I suspect they have to do with selflessness and selfishness, spiritual truth, humility, honor and love.

But that is only an unverified opinion. Or maybe it's a hope, because we are all capable of accomplishing those steps. Which means there is hope for everyone to experience the magic of the Gold Zone.

But I know for a fact that it's possible for everyone to achieve Mastery of something. Thereby experiencing the almost magical Green Zone.

Are you ready to find UP?

Recommended Reading

Life 101 by John-Roger and Peter McWilliams

The Secrets to Increasing Your Power, Wealth, and Happiness by Alan C. Walter

The Power of Now by Eckhart Tolle

The Seven Habits of Highly Effective People by Steven Covey

Illusions by Richard Bach

Rich Dad, Poor Dad by Robert Kiyosaki

The Cashflow Quadrant by Robert Kiyosaki

The Power of Positive Thinking by Norman Vincent Peale

Think and Grow Rich by Napoleon Hill

Recommended Videos

What The Bleep Do We Know? (1st edition)

What Dreams May Come

The Secret

About the Author

Linda Anthony Hill is originally from Central Florida. She spent most of her life working in the dental laboratory industry. In fact, she retired having Mastered dental technology. Over the course of that forty-five-year career. Linda was President and CEO, for thirty-five years, of her own dental lab corporation with over 15 employees in their hay-day.

She published her first book before retiring from dentistry and has been writing ever since. Her preferred genre is Paranormal Mystery. She even has a children's paranormal series. Her paranormal cozy mystery, THE ANCHOR IS THE KEY has won two awards for literary fiction. THE SPIDER HOUSE has only been released a few months at this writing, so no awards yet. Yet.

What most people don't know about Linda is that she has spent decades studying people, and what makes them tick. Raised a Catholic in the fifties and sixties, she sought more. More spirit, less religion. She found many answers along the way. She has taken courses in everything from management to communication to Yoga to coaching and leadership, and more.

You can find her other books at amazon.com/author/hilllin or on her website at www.LindaAnthonyHill.com She looks forward to reading your comments on this book and all her books on Amazon, as well.

Please share this with a friend. Having someone to share this information with makes it so much easier to accomplish.